Dedicated to all the great dads and bonus dads out there!

To my husband, Daniel, for supporting my dreams and to my bonus dad, Robin, for always being there for me!

Meet June
Text and Illustrations copyright ©2022 by April Martin

Calendar Kids Books, LLC | Kathleen, GA 31047

ISBN: 978-1-957161-03-7 (Paperback), 978-1-957161-04-4 (Hardback), 978-1-957161-05-1 (Ebook)
Library of Congress Control Number: 2022902097

All rights reserved. No part of this publication may be used or reproduced in any manner, electronic or mechanical, including photocopying, recording, or any information storage or retrieval system, without prior written permission from the publisher.

To find out more about The Calendar Kids Series visit www.calendarkidsbooks.com and sign up for newsletters.

The Calendar Kids
Meet June

April Martin

This is June.

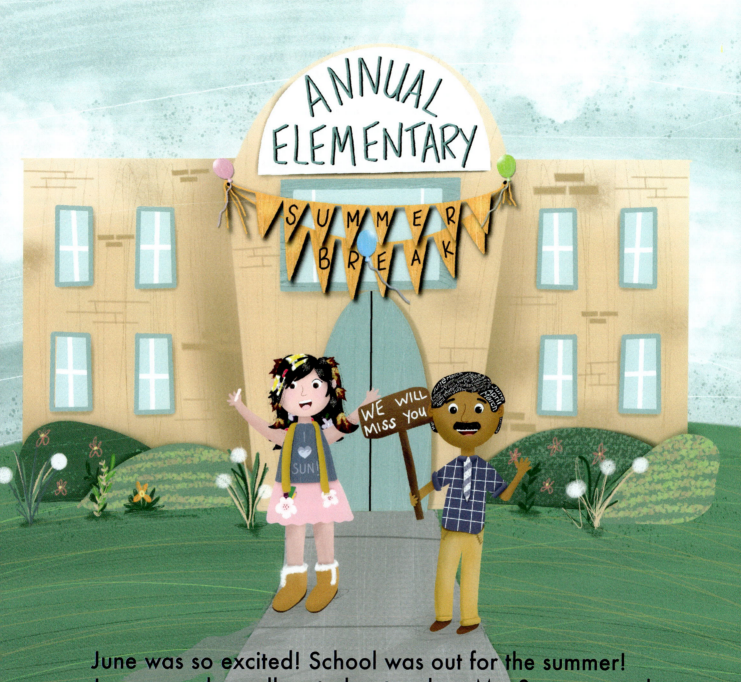

June was so excited! School was out for the summer! June waved goodbye to her teacher, Ms. Seasons, and the principal, Mr. Cal Endar.

June loves the warm summer days, but most of all she loves the summer trips her family plans each year.

One year they went to the mountains, another year they went on a cruise to an island, last year they went on a trip to ride rollercoasters!

This year, June's family planned a fun trip to the beach to celebrate Father's Day.

Before they left for their summer trip, June spent her days playing with her closest friends, May and July. It was their tradition to start the summer off with a water play day!

Sandy, her pet hermit crab, loved to play with them too!

May, June, and July also loved to go to summer camps together. At the beginning of the summer they went to art camp! They used their imaginations to create fun pieces of art.

While at art camp, May, June, and July also made Father's Day cards.

May made a card for her grandpa,

June made a card for her dad,

and July made a card for his stepdad.

June was thrilled with her card. It was perfect! June couldn't wait to give it to her dad for Father's Day!

The only thing June had left to do was to come up with a gift to give him! Last year she gave him a mug. He loves his coffee! The year before that, she gave him an apron to wear while he grilled burgers.

This year, she just couldn't decide what to do for her dad.

The day of their family trip finally came. After June made a checklist and packed her bags, she was ready for their beach adventure.

Sandy packed his shells too!

On the drive to the beach, June thought of gifts for her dad.

I could give him a pet crab! No...

I could give him a new pair of swim trunks, but I don't know his size.

"I know!" June thought. "I am going to build him the **biggest** sandcastle at the beach!"

First, June had to come up with a plan. She thought of everything she needed to make a sandcastle.

She needed...

a shovel,

a bucket,

a castle mold,

shells for decorations,

and water.

On the first day of the trip an afternoon summer storm swept through and it rained... not the best day to build a sandcastle.

On the second day the rain finally stopped and June spent so long in the pool she totally forgot to get started!

"It's a beautiful sandcastle," she thought...

... until the tide washed it all away.

My house...

"Oh nooo, this is harder than I thought it would be," June sighed. "I will just have to give him my card." June slowly walked back to the hotel room to get her card from art camp ready for Father's Day...

… But it was nowhere to be found. June realized she left it at home. "I have nothing for Daddy now," she cried. June was so sad. She wanted her dad to know how much she loved him.

That night, while she was laying awake in bed, June decided to come up with another plan...

She thought...

...and she thought...

...and she thought.

"AH-HA!"

"Tomorrow I will make Daddy something even more special!"

Instead of a sandcastle, June created a note in the sand. She used what she had with driftwood, seashells, seaweed, and starfish.

She placed the last shell and it was wonderful!
"Nothing will destroy this!" June said with glee.
"It is perfect! It is a note and a gift!"

"Daddy, Daddy, I have something for you! Close your eyes..." June shouted in excitement on Father's Day morning.

That afternoon they made June's favorite, her dad's famous burgers! They spent all day playing on the beach and building sandcastles together.

"This is the best trip ever!" June thought.

As they drove home, June could feel the warm summer air blowing through the car. She wondered what they would plan for next year's trip. Most of all, June could not wait to get home and hear what special things May and July did for Father's Day.

The next day, May told June all about how she spent the day with her grandpa who told stories about her dad.

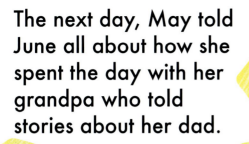

July told June about the crazy camping trip he went on with his stepdad.

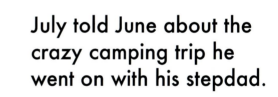

May, June, and July all laughed at the stories they shared. "What a great start to summer," June cheered.

My June Notebook

Special June birthdays or events in my family:

The best part about the month of June is...

June Fun Facts

- June is the 6th month of the year.
- The month after June is July.
- The first day of summer officially starts between June 20th-22nd each year.
- Great American Picnic Day is on June 25th.
- Father's Day in the USA is always the 3rd Sunday of the month.
- History in June: Juneteenth (June 19th) commemorates the end of slavery in the USA.
- If you are born in June your birthstone is Alexandrite.
- The month of June has 30 days.

Discussion Questions

1. What is the name of the elementary school? What does the word "annual" mean?

2. May, June, and July made cards for different family members for Father's Day. Who do you make cards for on special days?

3. June loves summer vacation. She packs her bags full of summer clothes. Name the clothes you wear during the summer.

4. June built a nice sandcastle! What happened to it? What does the word "tide" mean?

5. When June came up with the idea to use shells for a message to her dad, the author used the word "glee" to describe how June spoke. What does the word "glee" mean?

6. What traditions does your family do on special days like Father's Day or on the last day of school?

7. Have you ever been to the beach? What activities did you do that were fun? If not, what would you like to do at the beach?

Visit www.calendarkidsbooks.com for more resources!

Dad's Famous Burger Recipe

You will need:

1 pound of ground beef, thawed
1 cup of shredded cheddar cheese
1/2 cup salsa
1/4 cup bread crumbs (optional)
1 package of hamburger or slider buns
Toppings: lettuce, sliced cheese, bacon, tomato, avocado, onions, or none!

Directions:

1. Wash your hands. Grab a large bowl and open the ground beef package. Place the beef in the large bowl.

2. Add the cheese and salsa to the bowl. Don't add the buns and toppings; that would be silly.

3. Using your hands, mix together the beef, salsa, and shredded cheese. This is the messy part!

4. Form a ball with a handful of the beef mixture. A big handful will make a hamburger, a small handful will make sliders. Flatten into a patty.

5. Place the hamburger patties on a tray and ask a grown up to cook the beef patty on a grill. Wash your hands!

4. Grab your favorite toppings while the burgers are cooking and put them on a plate or in a bowl. Some grownups like to load it up with toppings like lettuce, cheese, bacon, tomatoes, and ketchup. Some kids do too!

5. When the hamburgers are finished cooking assemble your hamburger. Grab a bun, put a patty on top, and add any topping of your choice.

meet APRIL

April Martin is a mother, military spouse, and teacher. While teaching her first grade class she discovered there were not many books to teach her students about the months of the year... that's where her very own name gave her an idea! She realized she could create characters named after the months of the year that her students could know and love. Time went by, LOTS of time, but her characters were still in her thoughts. Now, a mother herself, she wanted to finally bring her "kids" to life. April knew all along the vision she had for her books and began to learn everything she could about writing and illustrating. April is a self-taught illustrator and always encourages others to explore new creative outlets. You never know, you could be just MONTHS away from creating something amazing!

I once had a pet hermit crab.

More Facts About April

"First things first... YES, I was born in April! Whew, glad that's over with."

"My favorite summer activity is watching the sunset at the beach."

"I LOVE to play in the sand. You can find me looking for shells or sand dollars too!"